G000038799

CAREFREE

HOW THE TITLE WAS WON

CAREFREE
HOW THE TITLE WAS WON

© Dave McCrossen

Dave McCrossen has asserted his rights in accordance with the Copyright,
Designs and Patents Act 1988 to be identified as the author of this work.

Publishing By:

Pitch Publishing (Brighton) Ltd
10 Beresford Court
Somerhill Road
Hove BN3 1RH
Email: info@pitchpublishing.co.uk
Web: www.pitchpublishing.co.uk

First published 2005.

All rights reserved. No part of this publication may be reproduced, stored in
a retrieval system, or transmitted in any form or by any means, electronic,
mechanical, photocopying, recording or otherwise, without the prior permission
in writing of the publisher and the copyright owners.

A catalogue record for this book is available from the British Library.

ISBN 0-9542460-7-1

All pictures by Dave McCrossen, except for the following:

Action Images: 1, 2, 3, 5, 6, 7, 9, 11, 16, 18, 21, 24, 27, 29, 31, 40, 41, 43,
44, 45, 48, 49, 50, 55, 56, 63, 64, 67, 69, 70, 72, 75, 76, 77, 79, 80
Bennett Dean: 85-90

Printed and bound in Great Britain by Cambridge University Press

Acknowledgements

I would like to thank Paul at Pitch whose idea this book was, and who has spent many a happy hour trying to make sense of the jumble of stuff I sent him.

Thanks are also due to John Terry's Barmy Army. They are Martin, so often buried in a chocolate cake; Peter, who hid my money from me in Barcelona; Ray, who wears an annoying hat in order to cover up an even more annoying haircut; Piers, who will doubtless be too drunk to read these words; and most of all Rue, for his contribution as number one train spotter!

Rose deserves a special mention for somehow managing to find time in between all of her other work to act as our unpaid travel agent; and Chris for being so understanding of my desire to follow Chelsea over land, sea and Leicester.

Finally, the obvious thanks go to Roman for giving us the money to make all our dreams come true; to José for bringing all those years of frustration to an end; to the team who - despite a few scares along the way - gave us an outfit of which we could be so very proud; and last, but by no means least, the true inspiration behind our travels and our team. The world's finest centre-back, John Terry.

Now all they have to do is to do it all again!

Introduction

Being a Chelsea fan has never been easy; so many times the team has flattered to deceive. Before the start of each season, for as long as I can recall, I have hoped, prayed and sometimes even believed a little that this would be our year. That all of those years of frustration, of long trips home following defeats to the likes of Rotherham United and Scunthorpe, were finally going to come to an end. This season, our season, those dreams finally came true in glorious Technicolor.

In so many ways, this season has been the most memorable one ever for me and thousands of other lifelong Blues fans. There was that glorious night against Barcelona where we could have beaten anyone (why did we stop at four?!) and that never-to-be-forgotten day at the Reebok in Bolton where all those years in the wilderness were finally forgotten when Frank Lampard took an age to run from the halfway line, round the keeper and bang the ball into the empty net.

A little over a season and a half ago, yet it seems like a lifetime, a number of us met up in a pub in Leicester shortly before stuffing the foxes. We were looking forward to a trip to Stuttgart at that point and decided, for no special reason, to dress up as vicars. We decided that people stupid enough to make themselves a laughing stock deserved to have a name, and thus John Terry's Barmy Army was born. JT always looks out for the flag and gives it a wave (not at home as our stewards won't allow it!) and his signature proudly takes up the centre of it.

The dressing up continues, but what has changed this season is the attitude and confidence of the team. Our journeys this season, always with camera in hand, have now become nothing but one long and very enjoyable memory. We had great results all over Europe, from a cakewalk in Paris to a demolition of Barcelona at Stamford Bridge. The one game that will live with me forever, though, will be our trip to Bolton Wanderers. Bolton is not exactly the most glamorous place in the world, but for about 5000 Chelsea fans on a sunny April afternoon it became a heaven on earth.

What follows is a pictorial history of Chelsea's greatest-ever season seen through the eyes of the now infamous Barmy Army. I hope that these photographs will help you remember each little twist and turn of the season that ended for us all in such a memorable way.

It has been a long time in coming. Savour every moment of being champions of England. I don't believe everything I am told, but I believe José when he says we will not be waiting 50 years for the next one!

David McCrossen
May 2005

"I have every part of me crossed that
this will finally be our season."

Chelsea fan Peter Wright

"I have read I have to prove a lot in English football. Sir Alex Ferguson is the only European champion in this country – nobody else – so I have to prove what?"

Chelsea manager José Mourinho

"Every time we go on the pitch and play you can see the spirit: the way we play, the way we work for each other. It's as plain as the nose on my face."

Chelsea assistant manager Steve Clarke

"I told Mr Ferguson United didn't
deserve to leave with nothing."

José Mourinho

"The whole history of football has been written by passionate men and rich men. They've put their heart and money into the game and this is the only way. The most important thing for a fan is money and passion and Chelsea have both. To develop a great history you have to start somewhere and that's what Chelsea are doing. It's good for football that there are new clubs emerging."

Juventus director Romy Gai

"I don't think we should lose sight of what José has achieved as a manager. I don't think he is an enemy of football. I think the opposite. He is a manager who is absolutely serious about his art. I have found Mourinho very respectful."

Crystal Palace manager Iain Dowie

"He comes from Portugal, he hates the Arsenal!"

Chelsea fans tribute to Tiago

"I wish I was playing now!"

Former blues captain Colin Pates

"He wants to annihilate the opposition, that's him. He's not happy with being nine, ten or even eleven points clear, he wants to keep winning and winning and winning. That's the only thing the man knows."

Chelsea captain John Terry

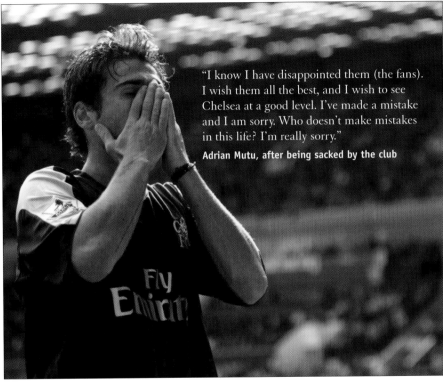

"I know I have disappointed them (the fans). I wish them all the best, and I wish to see Chelsea at a good level. I've made a mistake and I am sorry. Who doesn't make mistakes in this life? I'm really sorry."

Adrian Mutu, after being sacked by the club

"When I met him at the beginning of July and he was with his two agents, I told them: 'I have information that Mutu is on cocaine'. All three of them were laughing – denying this – saying that there were a lot of big lies about Adrian. Maybe some because last season he had some strange behaviour in the club and in his social life, but it is completely untrue and he wants to start from the first day over. After that, I didn't speak with him again because they denied the situation."

José Mourinho

"Flares and flag poles are strictly forbidden."

Sign outside of Paris Saint Germain's ground

"I'm just so excited. I can't stop looking at the fixture list and thinking if we win this game, this game and this game, then... But it's important to check yourself and just think about winning the next game."

Chelsea's Joe Cole

"I am frustrated because there is only one team that played to win and the other just not to concede goals. They had a header and then defended, they didn't play football, they brought the bus and left the bus in front of the goal, as we say in my country."

José Mourinho after the 0-0 home draw against Tottenham

"There are a lot of players at Porto who are my players but there are no friends during the 90 minutes."

José Mourinho

"We played a good game against a very good team. The only thing is when you keep the ball and you are counter-attacking, you need to score."

Liverpool manager Rafael Benitez

"The new City of Manchester Stadium has cost £135million to build."

The BBC's website

"The manager drums it into us to that we should win every game and in the dressing room afterwards he was telling us to forget the defeat as soon as possible and start focusing on the next league game."

John Terry after the Manchester City defeat

"We were missing two key players and the final pass just wasn't good enough and there were two, maybe three, occasions when you have to say Chelsea defended extremely well."

CSKA Moscow coach Valery Gazzaev

"I was a reluctant leaver. I'd been at the club a long time and I loved the place – I still do."

Blues legend Clive Walker

"The goals against column doesn't lie – it is quite obvious where our problems lie."

Blackburn manager Mark Hughes

"We must be doing something right as everyone seems to keep having a go at us!"

Chelsea fan Rue Preston

"You're going down with the Tottenham!"

Chelsea fans' taunt to WBA supporters

"Job done. As simple as that."

Chelsea fan Kevin Foot

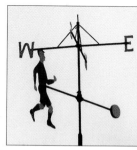

"If I had twelve million pounds I would buy a player like that – but the fact is we can't shop at Armani so we have to shop at Marks and Spencer's instead."

Everton manager David Moyes talking about Arjen Robben

"I said three years ago that Robben is a small phenomenon in Holland and he will be a big phenomenon. There are maybe two or three players as good as he is in the last 20 or 30 years. He's that good."

Tottenham manager Martin Jol

"We have just been beaten by the Champions."

Fulham manager Chris Coleman after the 4-1 victory at Craven Cottage

"I truly believe football at the top end has gone soft. For me, there is no greater sight than seeing the look on defenders' faces when they have been battered by Kevin Davies."

Bolton manager Sam Allardyce

"I think John Terry is an awesome talent."

Blues legend Alan Hudson

"I love everything about John Terry. I think you could call me a John Terry nut!"

Chelsea fan Beth Wilde

'I'm happy for the points, I'm happy for the result, the team, the attitude and our determination."

José Mourinho

"They say that class is permanent, and we showed that in bucketfuls today."

Chelsea fan Kevin Foot

"We will make sure Mourinho has a warm welcome - we are planning something special."

FC Porto fan Rui Teixeira

"Relieved? Yes of course. We deserved this victory. Little by little gaps opened up and we showed in this match we have the willingness to win, even if it wasn't easy."

FC Porto coach Victor Fernandez

"The whistle doesn't need to be blown. I asked Henry 'do you want a wall?'. He said 'can I take it please?' He was very polite. I said 'yes'."

Referee Graham Pol
on 'that' free kick

"I've seen them play a lot. I'm very happy for them because I know the club wanted to achieve this result, and for the supporters too. Obviously they invested a lot of money in the past two years, but they've also done all the things right. Chelsea are not only one of the best teams in England but in Europe too."

Blues legend Gianfranco Zola

"I've broken the metatarsal bone. I thought maybe I could run it off but it got worse so I had an X-ray on Saturday night and the bad news was I've broken my foot. The boss said to come off but I wanted to carry on. Everyone knows my situation and I just wanted to impress. If I can be back in late February, early March I will be really happy."

Chelsea's Scott Parker after injuring his foot against Norwich in December. It was his last performance of the season.

"We are loving it at the top and we're not feeling the pressure."

**Chelsea's Damien Duff
after scoring the winning goal**

"My Christmas message to the fans is that family is much more important than football. Don't care about football and don't worry about Chelsea being first, second or third or less. Don't be worried about winning or losing. Be worried about the people you love, the world and peace. These things are much more important than football."

José Mourinho when asked about the heavy Christmas schedule

"I feel gutted for Carlo as he has never let us down. But this fella is awesome!"

Chelsea fan Gary Taylor

"People don't like the fact that he says what he thinks. When he came here, he was quite controversial and there was a lot of criticism that he was buying expensive players. Now people do not like it when they see what he is doing is working and that Chelsea are one of the best teams in Europe. I went to him after the Carling Cup and after my goal against West Brom because I wanted to show my support and that when someone in our group is attacked, the whole team is attacked."

Chelsea's Didier Drogba speaking about life under José Mourinho

"When the score was 1-1 there was some nervy play from Chelsea and it was disappointing for Andy to score the own-goal. But we had our chances to equalise. Cleveland Taylor had a volley brilliantly saved by their goalkeeper and then he hit the post. We were pressing for the equaliser and then the third goal killed us. Their manager made a few changes and maybe that was the reason we started so well."

Scunthorpe United manager Brian Laws
after their 3-1 defeat in the FA Cup

"We tried everything to try and open them up. We played better than them in the first half hour and we still had the initiative in the second half but we weren't powerful enough up front. That was the only thing that disappointed me because we kept Arjen Robben quiet and Chelsea are the best team in the country."

Martin Jol

"I thought it was a penalty as well as the one before that and we could have had one in the second half. It was a difficult game for us because Tottenham were full of confidence. It's for other people to say whether it's our title to lose. We need to focus on our next match. There's not much other teams can do if you keep getting three points. We are not invincible."

Steve Clarke

"I think Mourinho's knowledge of the game is unbelievable. He is a great tactician, gives players belief in themselves and buys good players too."

Chelsea legend Peter Osgood

"There have been teams in the Premier League in recent seasons who have been eight or ten points clear but have still been caught."

Portsmouth's Joe Jordan after defeat against the Blues

FINALS   ROVERS   1   45   9:0
WEAR   CHELSEA   0

"I was upset that the opposing manager was not gracious enough to shake my hand. Sometimes you have to be gracious in defeat but you also have to be gracious in victory. I have no idea why. Perhaps he was too busy on the field with his players. Whether or not he was upset because they were not allowed to play the kind of football they wanted to play I don't know, but we did not overstep the mark, absolutely not."

Mark Hughes

"If people see losing one game as a blip, well that could happen to anybody on any day. But if a blip is losing two or three games on the spin - you can't see it happening at Chelsea."

Joe Cole after the 0-0 home draw against Manchester City

"I could not be as confident if I did not have that confidence in my players. When I say I think we are going to win the Premiership, it is not a lack of respect for Manchester United, Arsenal, or the 11 teams we have to play against, it is just our inside mentality. We are going to do it."

José Mourinho

"I'm sure that Barcelona will reach the quarter-finals. My predictions would be Real Madrid, Bayern Munich, or AC Milan and maybe Inter to challenge. I don't think any of the English sides will do it."

Barcelona's Ronaldinho

"Barca have the best attackers, but we have the best defence."

Chelsea's Mateja Kezman

"Did I touch him? Did I touch him? No, I never!"

Didier Drogba after being sent off

"I've met José but I don't know him well. I don't know how he works on the training pitch but I understand his players love him. That's great for him and, of course, you see the results of that on the pitch."

England Coach Sven-Goran Eriksson

"José Frisked."

Daily Mail back page headline after the 2-1 defeat in the Camp Nou

"Mourinho doesn't know how to lose."

A headline in one Spanish newspaper and perhaps the reason Chelsea hired him

"We got a lot of bad luck because Bridge was out after two minutes, then Duff got a kick after 10 minutes, so we played with nine people for the whole second half. It was very difficult, and then Carlo got the red card. It was a strange game and we are out of the competition."

Mateja Kezman

"It is a major Cup final and Chelsea will be the hot favourites. But I just think if Liverpool have a really good go at them, especially up front with Fernando Morientes and Milan Baros, you never know what will happen."

Liverpool legend Alan Hansen

"Winning the Carling Cup was very important to us. Everyone knows we want to win everything but that's not always possible... Between now and the end of the season, we can have the time of our lives. Five years was too long for modern Chelsea not to be winning silverware. We put an end to that. Now for the rest of this season, five weeks will be too long for us to go without winning anything."

John Terry

"The score might have been close but the gulf in class was a chasm!"

Chelsea fan Martin Swan

"Chelsea controlled the game when they started playing."

Rafael Benitez

"This is a new club, with a new manager and it is fantastic to get that first trophy out of the way."

Damien Duff

We came to the Millennium Stadium and we've shut people up. People started talking and underestimating us but it was a great win for us and, hopefully, that will stop them talking for a bit."

ohn Terry

Credit to Chelsea, they deserved the win and we have got to pick ourselves up, we've got other things to play for. But it is tough to take."

iverpool's Steven Gerrard after the defeat

"Was that gesticulation? All I saw was José pu
his fingers to his lips... it was fairly innocuous,

Frank Clark, the League Managers' Association

"We talked about José being here for 10 year
when he first came. We told him we want him
to stay that long. He is undoubtedly the bes
manager in the Premiership, he is exceptional.

Chelsea Chief Executive Peter Kenyo

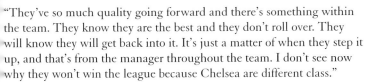

"They've so much quality going forward and there's something within the team. They know they are the best and they don't roll over. They will know they will get back into it. It's just a matter of when they step it up, and that's from the manager throughout the team. I don't see now why they won't win the league because Chelsea are different class."
Norwich City's Leon McKenzie

"You're going down with the soufflés!"

Chelsea fans' taunt to Norwich City supporters

"It was a really tough game. It is always nice to score but the most important thing was we got the three points. The team spirit is fantastic and I think that is what is keeping us going."

Joe Cole

I think José Mourinho has been a breath of fresh air for the English game."

Norwich City manager Nigel Worthington

"The whole world seems to think that Chelsea are invincible and the best team in Europe, but I want to help Barca prove that is not true. The major difference between the two sides is in scoring goals. Chelsea win with little effort up front, but we win with loads of goals and there will be no doubt we are superior after these two games."

Barcelona's Samuel Eto'o before their 4-2 defeat at Stamford Bridge

"Lampard would really fit in well in the Barcelona team. He would make Barcelona stronger in midfield."

Barcelona legend Johan Cruyff

"It was 19 minutes gone and I'm thinking: "Oh my God, we're 3-0 up against Barcelona. What's happening here?" I didn't know if I was dreaming."

Chelsea's Eidur Gudjohnsen

UEFA CHAMPIONS LEAGUE

77:28

5-4

4 - 2

GUDJOHNSEN 8
LAMPARD 17
...FF 19
...RY 76

RONAL'HO
27, 38

FCB

AC MILAN 1-0 MAN UTD

"If Chelsea win the European Cup it would be laughable. They are not a good team, they scored three quick goals because we let them, but the referee was very lenient to them."

Barcelona's Samuel Eto'o after their 4-2 defeat

"I just hope our players have looked at the reports over the weekend where Mourinho and Terry say they are not content at just beating teams but want to annihilate them. That is an insult."

West Bromwich Albion manager Bryan Robson before the game

"I just can't see Chelsea losing three or four games between now and the end of the season. I think Chelsea are more or less there now."

Bryan Robson after the game

"All the clubs want at the lower level is to be respected. I understand Bryan Robson made some comments about him [Mourinho], but I've found him very amiable, very passionate and steeled with desire to make his team win."

Crystal Palace manager Iain Dowie

"We will go in there and mix it up, get them on the backfoot, get in their faces and stop them from playing. We are determined to let them know they haven't been in an easy game."

Crystal Palace's Emmerson Boyce

"The scoreline was probably harsh but you can't defend like we did for the second and fourth goals. We shouldn't have let Joe Cole get in there for their second goal. Manchester United, Arsenal and Chelsea are all good sides, but Chelsea are capable of beating you in different ways. Now the other two have everything to do to catch them."

Iain Dowie

"The biggest difference José has made this season is in the confidence level. The confidence he has breathed into the team is amazing. We can still improve and he is a perfectionist. He wants to win every game and every tournament we take part in. I think that winning mentality has been the biggest difference. When he keeps going on TV saying we are going to win the league, maybe it is something the players needed to hear from their manager. "

Eidur Gudjohnsen

"Considering where we used to train, the old place really held us back because it just wasn't a nice place to be. It was hard to keep your focus when the going got really tough. Now they are pampered to the highest level and that's great. I think they've got a chance to be successful again. They've certainly got the title won this year. I've no doubt."

Graeme Le Saux

"There was very little in it. They never opened us up but they are a good side and that's why they will win the title. In the end, a bad free-kick made all the difference."

Harry Redknapp

"When I arrived, I had to put up with the transfer fee and the expectations that go with it. I also had to adapt to a new environment. It was a little heavy to bear and, just when I was starting to digest it all, I got a hamstring injury. I was scoring regularly at the time."

Didier Drogba

"I was thinking with ten minutes to go, can we be the first team to get a win here? That would have been special, but it was not to be."

Steve Bruce

"Two goals is a good lead although three would have been better. We are in a good position for the second leg and we feel we can score anywhere."

Frank Lampard

"We feel fantastic, we couldn't be better. We have trophy, we're top of the league, we're in the quarter-finals of the Champions League and we won the first game."

José Mourinho

"We go into the game convinced we can knock Chelsea out."

Bayern Munich Coach Felix Magath

"I didn't create any problems for Uefa. I respected their decision to ban me for two games even if I didn't think it was at all fair."

José Mourinho

If I wanted to have an easy job I would have stayed at Porto. Beautiful blue chair, the UEFA Champions League Trophy, God, and after God, me."

José Mourinho

First of all I think it is fantastic that we are in the semi-finals. I think we were the better team over the two games. The most important thing is that we are in the semi-finals. Everybody has done a fantastic job. We are delighted. I didn't speak with José during the game. I think he watched the game at the hotel. His idea was to watch the match from the stands but I think he decided that he didn't have the privacy to do it and so he went back to the hotel."

Chelsea fitness coach Rui Faria gives the Blues view at the post-match press conference

"It would have been nice to beat Arsenal for a change, maybe we wil reserve that pleasure for next season when we retain the title.

Chelsea Fan Ian Colema

"After 32 games, there is no coincidence. You have to respect what Chelsea have done on the pitch. They are 11 points better so that means there was a gap this year. But it is not over yet, we have a chance to close the gap and then there are five games to go. I don't feel it personally but the points tell the story. Contrary to the European Cup, where anything can happen, there are no coincidences in the league."

Arsenal manager Arsene Wenger

"When Arsenal played Chelsea last month I went to Stamford Bridge and sat in the Matthew Harding Stand. Opposite a snack bar there's a giant picture of me diving for a header. I saw it and stopped in my tracks, my spine tingling. All the success they're experiencing and they've got a photo of me on the wall? It made me realise how lucky I was to play for this great club. I always felt Chelsea could be something special. Now they are."

Tony Cascarino

"It was 50 years ago to the day that we last lifted the title, and we are all but there now. Football does come up with some amazing tricks of fate."

Chelsea fan Ian Coleman

"I had a tour of Old Trafford, the training ground and met Mr Ferguson, but the two clubs could not come to an agreement. Then Chelsea began showing a lot of interest. As soon as I arrive I instantly had a great feeling, it filled me with confidence and it was clear I had to decide to come to Chelsea - no doubt about it. Since then I've had no regrets at all. I'm really happy here and I've settled in well."

Arjen Robben

"I do not want to win the league on Monday. I am hoping Arsenal can beat Tottenham and I want to put this mentality on to my players. If we win the league on Monday it is possible we could lose at Bolton next Saturday. I don't want to do that. If we need a result there I prefer to get it."

José Mourinho

"Have you ever seen Chelsea win the League? YES WE HAVE!"

Chelsea fans at Bolton

"I think just him being here (Roman Abramovich) shows his enthusiasm for us and the club. It is not just a hobby, it is something he puts his heart into. He is a fan of football and a big fan of Chelsea. It's definitely the proudest moment of my career, if not my whole life.

Eidur Gudjohnsen

"What can I say. What a day. A day that will stay with me for the rest of my life. I feel so honoured and privileged that I was at the game and able to watch such a momentous moment in my life."

Chelsea fan Steve Lewis

"This is fantastic. I can't put it into words, it's what we play for. There was a point when I thought that but I can't believe what has happened now. It's fantastic, just different class. It's what you play for and I can't believe it. Can we make it three trophies in a season? Why not? We're going to be flying now."

Joe Cole

"It is the best feeling ever. It's been a long time coming, the supporters have been waiting a long time and they fully deserve it. We did not start too well in the first half and we got a bit of a telling off. The response was perfect. It is so special, the lads and everyone deserve this. It's been fantastic."

John Terry

"I agree money doesn't buy points and victories, If you go back a few months Porto, with 10 percent of Man United's budget, beat them. Money buys players but not a team."

José Mourinho

"This is a personal award, but the main one I won this season was the Premiership - and I could not have done that without the players around me. Everyone has seen how strong we are this year and I would like to say thanks to all of them - and also a massive thank you to all the Chelsea fans. They took me to their hearts very, very quickly and I have nothing but appreciation for them. They give me the confidence to be the player I am today. They are a piece of my heart now and I really mean that."

**Frank Lampard when picking up his
Footballer Of The Year Award**

"Game over, we really are CHAMPIONS. We were there weren't we? I don't want to wake up if it was a dream."

Chelsea fan Neil Holmes

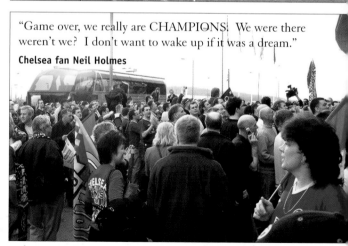

"I couldn't tell from where I wa
but a few of the lads said the ba
didn't go over the line. Willian
Gallas was in the way of the ba
from where the linesman wa
but he gave it - which was a ba
decision. If you're not sure, the
don't give a goal.

John Terr

"We were one match from the final. Why couldn't we get there? You shouldn't be tired with just one match remaining to be played. We should have played with our hearts and minds. That had been our strong point all season. Not this time."

Willliam Gallas

"What can I say? Just that the best team lost. No doubt, that is for sure. The best team didn't deserve to lose. But football is sometimes cruel and you have to accept the reality. Sometimes it goes for you and sometimes it goes against you. They scored, if you can say that they scored, because maybe you should say the linesman scored. They were 1-0 up and, after that, they just defended. They did it well, with a lot of courage, commitment and enthusiasm."

José Mourinho

"It has been a long time coming, but I would have waited for this moment forever!"

A Chelsea fan queuing to get into the Charlton game

"If Roman Abramovich helped me out in training we would be bottom of the league and if I had to work in his world of big business, we would be bankrupt!"

José Mourinho

"I always knew we would win it one day. Other teams can sing about their sides being, 'by far the greatest team', but we know it is true of only one side."

Chelsea fan Margaret Helsey

"We want to do this for as long as we can. There is no reason why we can't do it again next year. We've got the players and the management."

Joe Cole

"The talk about the pressure on us to defend the title has already started. But we have been under pressure for the whole of this season and we managed to withstand it. It is difficult to predict things in football, but I believe we will compete for the top places the next season as well."

Petr Cech

"I could talk about him all day long. He has been doing brilliantly for Chelsea – I have certainly never seen him play so well. I have always known what a great player he was, it was just important for him to get a run in the team."

John Terry talking about Joe Cole

"I think he has enjoyed it. It's not an easy league to get involved in for your first year in English football. The Premier division is very difficult so I think he has deserved his title. They have done very, very well and they are a very good, powerful team."

Sir Alex Ferguson on José Mourinho in his end-of-term report

"I think it's the perfect way to beat the record in such an amazing stadium against big Man United, against a team which has in Sir Alex a big example of success and fair play."

José Mourinho

"There will be no cheap Portuguese plonk in the manager's office tonight, but there will be a fine wine deserving of a champion, and I will not hesitate to raise my glass and toast José Mourinho's success."

Sir Alex Ferguson

"Chelsea broke the Premier League points record held by Manchester United when they beat them 3-1 at Old Trafford on Tuesday. The English champions came from behind to notch their 29th win of the season and lead the standings on 94 points with one match to go. United set the previous record of 92 in the 1993-94 season. Chelsea can set another modern-era record in their 38th and last match at Newcastle United on Sunday. They have only conceded 14 goals to Liverpool's 16 in 1978-79, over 42 games."

Reuters News Agency

"Chelsea come here today as worthy champions. They've been fantastic all season and after a lot of 1-0 wins early in the season their confidence grew and they started knocking in a lot of goals. Now they're the great entertainers and the team everybody wants to see."

Newcastle manager Graeme Souness

"That's why, we're the Champions."

Chelsea fans after Frank Lampard equalised at St James' Park

"Our group is a special group, they deserve this - nobody can say we don't deserve this. We were absolutely magnificent, the players and the fans. I want to stay with Chelsea as long as I can. My heart is with the club."

José Mourinho

CHELSEA

BARCLAYS PREMIERSHIP CHAMPIONS

CHELSEA

FOOTBALL CLUB

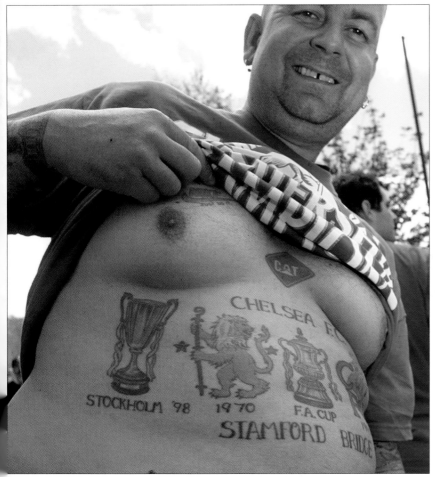

"Players around the world will see this parade on television and want to be part of this club. There are some massive clubs in this country and Chelsea are now firmly one of those teams. All you can see is a sea of blue and white and very, very happy faces. The players have done their job and now they can relax and enjoy it. People claimed they were just here for the money but it was great to see all the foreign lads getting into the celebrations. You could see how much it meant to them."

Blues legend John Hollins

The season record
2004/2005

FA PREMIERSHIP 2004/2005

15/08	**CHELSEA 1 MANCHESTER UNITED 0**	41813
H	Goalscorer: Gudjohnsen 15 Cech, Gallas, Ferreira, Terry, Bridge, Lampard, Geremi (Carvalho 89) Makelele, Smertin, Drogba (Kezman 70), Gudjohnsen (Parker 82) Unused Substitutes: Cudicini, Mutu	Graham Poll
21/08	**BIRMINGHAM CITY 0 CHELSEA 1**	28559
A	Goalscorer: Cole 68 Cech, Carvalho, Ferreira, Terry, Bridge, Lampard, Geremi (Cole 63), Makelele, Smertin (Tiago 45), Drogba, Gudjohnsen (Kezman 45) Unused Substitutes: Cudicini, Gallas	Barry Knight
24/08	**CRYSTAL PALACE 0 CHELSEA 2**	24953
A	Goalscorers: Drogba 28; Tiago 72 Cech, Ferreira, Gallas, Terry, Babayaro, Lampard, Cole (Geremi 76), Makelele, Tiago, Drogba (Gudjohnsen 75), Kezman (Mutu 70) Unused Substitutes: Cudicini, Carvalho	Chris Foy
28/08	**CHELSEA 2 SOUTHAMPTON 1**	40864
H	Goalscorers: Beattie 34 (og); Lampard 41 (pen) Cech, Carvalho, Ferreira, Terry, Bridge, Lampard, Cole (Duff 57), Makelele (Geremi 90), Tiago, Drogba, Gudjohnsen (Kezman 60) Unused Substitutes: Pidgeley, Gallas	Steve Bennett
11/09	**ASTON VILLA 0 CHELSEA 0**	36691
A	Cech, Ferreira, Carvalho, Babayaro, Terry, Lampard, Cole (Mutu 61), Makelele, Tiago (Smertin 66), Drogba, Kezman (Gudjohnsen 61) Unused Substitutes: Pidgeley, Gallas	Rob Styles
19/09	**CHELSEA 0 TOTTENHAM HOTSPUR 0**	42246
H	Cech, Ferreira, Carvalho, Terry, Bridge (Smertin 85), Lampard, Cole (Duff 66), Makelele, Tiago (Kezman 66), Drogba, Gudjohnsen Unused Substitutes: Pidgeley, Gallas	Mike Riley

25/09	MIDDLESBROUGH 0 CHELSEA 1	32341
A	Goalscorer: Drogba 81 Cech, Carvalho, Ferreira, Terry, Gallas, Smertin (Tiago 65), Duff (Huth 88), Lampard, Makelele, Drogba, Gudjohnsen (Kezman 65) Unused Substitutes: Pidgeley, Cole	Mark Halsey
3/10	CHELSEA 1 LIVERPOOL 0	42028
H	Goalscorer: Cole 64 Cech, Ferreira, Terry, Carvalho, Gallas, Makelele, Smertin (Tiago 85), Lampard, Duff (Geremi 81), Drogba (Cole 38), Gudjohnsen Unused Substitutes: Cudicini, Huth	Phil Dowd
16/10	MANCHESTER CITY 1 CHELSEA 0	45047
A	Cech, Ferreira, Terry, Carvalho (Geremi 78), Gallas (Bridge 45), Tiago (Cole 64), Lampard, Makelele, Duff, Kezman, Gudjohnsen Unused Substitutes: Parker, Cudicini	Howard Webb
23/10	CHELSEA 4 BLACKBURN ROVERS 0	41546
H	Goalscorers: Gudjohnsen 37, 38, 51 (pen); Duff 74 Cech, Johnson, Carvalho, Terry, Bridge, Smertin (Tiago 65), Parker, Lampard, Cole (Robben 63), Duff, Gudjohnsen (Kezman 72) Unused Substitutes: Gallas, Cudicini	Graham Poll
30/10	WEST BROMWICH ALBION 1 CHELSEA 4	27399
A	Goalscorers: Gallas 45; Gudjohnsen 51; Duff 59; Lampard 81 Cech, Ferreira, Terry, Gallas, Bridge (Carvalho 46), Smertin, Makelele, Lampard (Tiago 83), Cole (Robben 46), Gudjohnsen, Duff Unused Substitutes: Kezman, Cudicini	Barry Knight
06/11	CHELSEA 1 EVERTON 0	41965
H	Goalscorer: Robben 72 Cech, Ferreira, Carvalho, Terry, Babayaro, Makelele, Lampard, Tiago (Kezman 58), Robben, Duff (Huth 82), Gudjohnsen (Geremi 78) Unused Substitutes: Cole, Cudicini	Mike Riley

13/11	**FULHAM 1 CHELSEA 4**	21877
A	Goalscorers: Lampard 33; Robben 59; Gallas 73; Tiago 81 Cech, Ferreira, Carvalho, Terry, Gallas, Smertin (Tiago 63), Makelele, Lampard, Duff (Kezman 76), Robben, Gudjohnsen (Huth 83) Unused Substitutes: Cudicini, Bridge	Uriah Renni
20/11	**CHELSEA 2 BOLTON WANDERERS 2**	42203
H	Goalscorers: Duff 1; Tiago 48 Cech, Ferreira, Carvalho, Terry, Gallas, Lampard, Makelele, Tiago, Duff (Kezman 80), Gudjohnsen (Johnson 81), Robben Unused Substitutes: Bridge, Parker, Cudicini	Dermot Gallagher
27/11	**CHARLTON ATHLETIC 0 CHELSEA 4**	26355
A	Goalscorers: Duff 4; Terry 47, 50; Gudjohnsen 59 Cech, Ferreira, Terry, Carvalho, Gallas, Tiago, Lampard, Makelele, Duff (Geremi 71), Robben (Babayaro 79), Gudjohnsen (Drogba 61) Unused Substitutes: Smertin, Cudicini	Mark Clattenburg
04/12	**CHELSEA 4 NEWCASTLE UNITED 0**	42328
H	Goalscorers: Lampard 63; Drogba 69; Robben 89; Kezman 90 (pen) Cech, Ferreira, Carvalho, Terry, Gallas (Bridge 61), Tiago (Kezman 61), Makelele, Lampard, Robben, Gudjohnsen (Drogba 45), Duff Unused Substitutes: Parker, Pidgeley	Rob Styles
12/12	**ARSENAL 2 CHELSEA 2**	38153
A	Goalscorers: Terry 17; Gudjohnsen 46 Cech, Ferreira, Terry, Carvalho (Drogba 46), Gallas, Duff, Tiago (Bridge 45), Makelele, Lampard, Robben, Gudjohnsen (Parker 77) Unused Substitutes: Kezman, Cudicini	Graham Pol
18/12	**CHELSEA 4 NORWICH CITY 0**	42071
H	Goalscorers: Duff 10; Lampard 34; Robben 44; Drogba 83 Cech, Ferreira, Terry, Gallas, Bridge, Lampard, Makelele, Tiago (Parker 76), Duff, Robben (Kezman 78), Gudjohnsen (Drogba 60) Unused Substitutes: Johnson, Cudicini	Mike Dean

26/12	CHELSEA 1 ASTON VILLA 0	41950
H	Goalscorer: Duff 30 Cech, Ferreira, Gallas, Terry, Bridge, Lampard, Makelele, Tiago, Duff (Smertin 80), Gudjohnsen (Drogba 66), Robben (Johnson 90) Unused Substitutes: Kezman, Cudicini	Peter Walton
28/12	**PORTSMOUTH 0 CHELSEA 2**	**20210**
A	Goalscorers: Robben 79; Cole 90 Cech, Ferreira, Gallas, Terry, Johnson, Duff, Makelele, Smertin (Cole 73), Lampard, Robben (Geremi 81), Drogba (Gudjohnsen 58) Unused Substitutes: Cudicini, Bridge	Alan Wiley
01/01	**LIVERPOOL 0 CHELSEA 1**	**43886**
A	Goalscorer: Cole 80 Cech, Ferreira, Terry, Gallas, Johnson, Tiago, Lampard, Makelele, Duff (Cole 76), Robben (Kezman 83), Gudjohnsen (Drogba 61) Unused Substitutes: Cudicini, Geremi	Mike Riley
04/01	**CHELSEA 2 MIDDLESBROUGH 0**	**40982**
H	Goalscorers: Drogba 15, 17 Cech, Ferreira, Terry, Gallas, Smertin (Johnson 50), Makelele, Lampard, Cole (Tiago 62), Duff, Robben, Drogba (Kezman 79) Unused Substitutes: Gudjohnsen, Cudicini	Steve Bennett
15/01	**TOTTENHAM HOTSPUR 0 CHELSEA 2**	**36105**
A	Goalscorer: Lampard 39 (pen), 90 Cech, Johnson, Terry, Gallas, Ferreira, Smertin (Jarosik 70), Lampard, Makelele, Robben, Duff (Cole 80), Drogba (Gudjohnsen 76) Unused Substitutes: Cudicini, Bridge	Graham Poll
22/01	**CHELSEA 3 PORTSMOUTH 0**	**42267**
H	Goalscorers: Drogba 15, 39; Robben 21 Cech, Ferreira, Gallas, Terry, Bridge, Lampard, Makelele, Cole, Robben (Kezman 75), Drogba (Gudjohnsen 65), Duff (Tiago 67) Unused Substitutes: Cudicini, Jarosik	Mike Riley

02/02	**BLACKBURN ROVERS 0 CHELSEA 1**	23414
A	Goalscorer: Robben 5 Cech, Ferreira, Gallas, Terry, Bridge, Tiago, Makelele, Lampard, Duff, Gudjohnsen (Kezman 82), Robben (Cole 11 (Jarosik 79)) Unused Substitutes: Johnson, Cudicini	Uriah Renni
06/02	**CHELSEA 0 MANCHESTER CITY 0**	42093
H	Cech, Ferreira, Gallas, Terry, Bridge, Jarosik (Tiago 56), Lampard, Makelele, Duff, Gudjohnsen, Kezman (Cole 63) Unused Substitutes: Johnson, Smertin, Cudicini	Howard Web
12/02	**EVERTON 0 CHELSEA 1**	40270
A	Goalscorer: Gudjohnsen 69 Cech, Ferreira, Gallas, Terry, Bridge, Cole (Jarosik 72), Tiago (Johnson 90), Makelele, Lampard, Duff (Carvalho 90), Gudjohnsen Unused Substitutes: Cudicini, Smertin	Mike Riley
05/03	**NORWICH CITY 1 CHELSEA 3**	24506
A	Goalscorers: Cole 22; Kezman 71; Carvalho 79 Cech, Johnson, Carvalho, Terry, Ferreira, Makelele, Lampard, Tiago (Kezman 67), Cole, Drogba (Gudjohnsen 67), Duff (Jarosik 73) Unused Substitutes: Cudicini, Huth	Mark Halsey
15/03	**CHELSEA 1 WEST BROMWICH ALBION 0**	41713
H	Goalscorer: Drogba 26 Cech, Ferreira, Terry, Huth, Gallas, Makelele, Cole (Kezman 86), Lampard, Duff (Smertin 90), Gudjohnsen (Jarosik 74), Drogba Unused Substitutes: Carvalho, Cudicini	Neale Barry
19/03	**CHELSEA 4 CRYSTAL PALACE 1**	41667
H	Goalscorers: Lampard 29; Cole 54; Kezman 78, 90 Cech, Ferreira, Terry, Carvalho, Johnson, Makelele, Cole, Lampard, Duff (Robben 74), Drogba (Tiago 63), Gudjohnsen (Kezman 77) Unused Substitutes: Cudicini, Huth	Phil Dowd

02/04	**SOUTHAMPTON 1 CHELSEA 3**	31949
A	Goalscorers: Lampard 22; Gudjohnsen 39, 83 Cech, Johnson, Huth, Terry, Gallas, Lampard, Makelele, Gudjohnsen, Duff (Jarosik 80), Kezman (Drogba 65), Cole (Tiago 45) Unused Substitutes: Cudicini, Carvalho	Mark Halsey
09/04	**CHELSEA 1 BIRMINGHAM CITY 1**	42031
H	Goalscorer: Drogba 82 Cech, Johnson (Jarosik 69), Huth, Terry, Gallas, Lampard, Smertin (Gudjohnsen 45), Cole, Duff, Tiago, Kezman (Drogba 45) Unused Substitutes: Carvalho, Cudicini	Chris Foy
20/04	**CHELSEA 0 ARSENAL 0**	41621
H	Cech, Johnson, Terry, Gallas, Carvalho, Cole (Tiago 79), Lampard, Makelele, Duff (Kezman 85), Gudjohnsen (Jarosik 90), Drogba Unused Substitutes: Cudicini, Huth	Steve Bennett
23/04	**CHELSEA 3 FULHAM 1**	42081
H	Goalscorers: Cole 17; Lampard 64; Gudjohnsen 87 Cech, Johnson, Carvalho, Terry, Huth (Jarosik 45), Makelele, Lampard, Cole (Robben 45), Duff, Drogba (Tiago 74), Gudjohnsen Unused Substitutes: Kezman, Cudicini	Alan Wiley
30/04	**BOLTON WANDERERS 0 CHELSEA 2**	27653
A	Goalscorers: Lampard 60, 76 Cech, Terry, Carvalho, Gallas, Geremi, Tiago, Makelele (Smertin 90), Lampard, Jarosik, Gudjohnsen (Cole 85), Drogba (Huth 65) Unused Substitutes: Cudicini, Kezman	Steve Dunn
07/05	**CHELSEA 1 CHARLTON ATHLETIC 0**	42065
H	Goalscorer: Makelele 90 Cudicini (Pidgeley 82), Johnson (Jarosik 67), Terry, Carvalho, Gallas, Makelele, Cole, Lampard, Tiago (Forssell 67), Geremi, Gudjohnsen Unused Substitutes: Huth, Kezman	Mike Riley

10/05	**MANCHESTER UNITED 1 CHELSEA 3**	67832
A	Goalscorers: Tiago 17; Gudjohnsen 61; Cole 82; Cudicini, Johnson (Jarosik 72), Carvalho, Huth, Gallas, Geremi, Tiago, Makelele, Lampard, Cole (Grant 90), Gudjohnsen (Morais 86) Unused Substitutes: Cech, Forssell	Graham Po▮
15/05	**NEWCASTLE UNITED 1 CHELSEA 1**	52326
A	Goalscorer: Lampard 35 (pen) Cudicini, Carvalho, Huth, Johnson, Geremi, Makelele, Jarosik (Watt 90), Tiago, Lampard, Cole (Morais 89), Gudjohnsen (Oliveira 84) Unused Substitutes: Cech, Grant	Howard Web▮

FA CUP 2004/2005

08/01	**THIRD ROUND: CHELSEA 3 SCUNTHORPE UNITED 1**	40019
H	Goalscorers: Kezman 26; Crosby (og) 58; Gudjohnsen 86 Cudicini, Johnson, Watt, Smertin, Cole, Tiago, Geremi (Ferreira 69), Morais, Gudjohnsen, Kezman (Robben 81), Drogba (Jarosik 68) Unused Substitutes: Pidgeley, Grant	Dermot Gallagher
30/01	**FOURTH ROUND: CHELSEA 2 BIRMINGHAM CITY 0**	40379
H	Goalscorers: Huth 6; Terry 80 Cudicini, Johnson, Huth, Terry, Bridge, Cole, Smertin, Jarosik, Duff (Robben 45), Gudjohnsen (Drogba 65), Kezman (Lampard 60) Unused Substitutes: Pidgeley, Geremi	Mike Dean
20/02	**FIFTH ROUND: NEWCASTLE UNITED 1 CHELSEA 0**	45740
A	Cudicini, Johnson, Gallas, Carvalho, Bridge, Jarosik, Smertin, Tiago (Gudjohnsen 45), Geremi (Lampard 45), Kezman, Cole (Duff 45) Unused Substitutes: Cech, Ferreira	Mark Halsey

	P	W	D	L	GF	GA	W	D	L	GF	GA	Pts	GD
Chelsea	38	14	5	0	35	6	15	3	1	37	9	95	+57
Arsenal	38	13	5	1	54	19	12	3	4	33	17	83	+51
Manchester United	38	12	6	1	31	12	10	5	4	27	14	77	+32
Everton	38	12	2	5	24	15	6	5	8	21	31	61	-1
Liverpool	38	12	4	3	31	15	5	3	11	21	26	58	+11
Bolton Wanderers	38	9	5	5	25	18	7	5	7	24	26	58	+5
Middlesbrough	38	9	6	4	29	19	5	7	7	24	27	55	+7
Manchester City	38	8	6	5	24	14	5	7	7	23	25	52	+8
Tottenham Hotspur	38	9	5	5	36	22	5	5	9	11	19	52	+6
Aston Villa	38	8	6	5	26	17	4	5	10	19	35	47	-7
Charlton Athletic	38	8	4	7	29	29	4	6	9	13	29	46	-16
Birmingham City	38	8	6	5	24	15	3	6	10	16	31	45	-6
Fulham	38	8	4	7	29	26	4	4	11	23	34	44	-8
Newcastle United	38	7	7	5	25	25	3	7	9	22	32	44	-10
Blackburn Rovers	38	5	8	6	21	22	4	7	8	11	21	42	-11
Portsmouth	38	8	4	7	30	26	2	5	12	13	33	39	-16
West Bromwich Albion	38	5	8	6	17	24	1	8	10	19	37	34	-25
Crystal Palace	38	6	5	8	21	19	1	7	11	20	43	33	-21
Norwich City	38	7	5	7	29	32	0	7	12	13	45	33	-35
Southampton	38	5	9	5	30	30	1	5	13	15	36	32	-21

LEAGUE CUP 2004/2005

27/10	**THIRD ROUND: CHELSEA 1 WEST HAM 0**	41774
H	Goalscorer: Kezman 57 Cudicini, Ferreira, Carvalho, Gallas, Babayaro, Geremi, Parker (Lampard 68), Tiago, Kezman, Robben (Gudjohnsen 82), Cole (Duff 64) Unused Substitutes: Cech, Huth	Andy D'Urs
10/11	**FOURTH ROUND: NEWCASTLE UNITED 0 CHELSEA 2 AET**	38055
A	Goalscorers: Gudjohnsen 100; Robben 112 Cudicini, Johnson, Terry, Gallas, Bridge, Ferreira, Tiago, Parker (Gudjohnsen 96), Duff (Robben 63), Cole (Lampard 66), Kezman Unused Substitutes: Cech, Huth	Steve Benne
30/11	**FIFTH ROUND: FULHAM 1 CHELSEA 2**	14531
A	Goalscorers: Duff 55; Lampard 88 Cudicini, Johnson, Carvalho, Terry, Bridge, Smertin, Makelele, Parker, Robben (Cole 62), Duff (Lampard 76), Drogba (Gudjohnsen 58) Unused Substitutes: Cech, Ferreira	Steve Dunn
12/01	**SEMI FINAL FIRST LEG: CHELSEA 0 MANCHESTER UNITED 0**	41492
H	Cudicini, Ferreira, Terry, Gallas, Bridge, Lampard, Makelele, Tiago (Kezman 66), Cole (Jarosik 75), Gudjohnsen (Drogba 45), Duff Unused Substitutes: Cech, Johnson	Neale Barry
26/01	**SEMI FINAL SECOND LEG: MANCHESTER UNITED 1 CHELSEA 2**	67000
A	Goalscorers: Lampard 29; Duff 85 Cech, Ferreira, Gallas, Terry, Bridge, Makelele, Lampard, Tiago, Robben (Cole 90), Drogba (Gudjohnsen 68), Duff (Jarosik 87) Unused Substitutes: Cudicini, Huth	Rob Styles
27/02	**FINAL: LIVERPOOL 2 CHELSEA 3 AET**	78000
Millennium Stadium	Goalscorers: Gerrard (og) 79; Drogba 107; Kezman 112 Cech, Ferreira, Carvalho, Terry, Gallas (Kezman 74), Jarosik (Gudjohnsen 45), Lampard, Makelele, Cole (Johnson 81), Drogba, Duff Unused Substitutes: Pidgeley, Tiago	Steve Benne

The UEFA Champions League
2004/2005

UEFA CHAMPIONS LEAGUE 2004/2005

14/09	GROUP H: PARIS ST GERMAIN 0 CHELSEA 3	40263
A	Goalscorers: Terry 29: Drogba 45, 75 Cech, Gallas, Ferreira, Terry, Bridge, Lampard, Cole (Geremi 70), Tiago, Makelele, Drogba (Duff 80), Gudjohnsen (Kezman 12) Unused Substitutes: Pidgeley, Ricardo Carvalho, Parker, Mutu	Manuel Meju González
29/09	GROUP H: CHELSEA 3 FC PORTO 1	39237
H	Goalscorers: Smertin 7; Drogba 50; Terry 70 Cech, Ferreira, Carvalho, Terry, Gallas, Smertin, Makelele, Lampard, Duff (Tiago 66), Gudjohnsen (Kezman 80), Drogba (Geremi 88) Unused Substitutes: Cudicini, Johnson, Cole, Huth	Herbert Fan
20/10	GROUP H: CHELSEA 2 CSKA MOSCOW 0	33945
H	Goalscorers: Terry 9; Gudjohnsen 45 Cech, Ferreira, Gallas, Terry, Bridge, Lampard, Duff (Cole 76), Smertin (Parker 84), Makelele, Kezman (Tiago 62), Gudjohnsen Unused Substitutes: Cudicini, Johnson, Carvalho, Geremi	Lubos Mich
02/11	GROUP H: CSKA MOSCOW 0 CHELSEA 1	20000
A	Goalscorer: Robben 24 Cech, Johnson, Terry, Carvalho, Gallas (Ferreira 54), Duff, Parker (Tiago 65), Lampard, Makelele, Robben, Gudjohnsen (Kezman 68) Unused Substitutes: Cudicini, Babayaro, Cole, Huth	Massimo De Santis
24/11	GROUP H: CHELSEA 0 PARIS ST GERMAIN 0	39626
H	Cudicini, Johnson, Carvalho, Gallas, Bridge, Smertin, Parker, Lampard (Gudjohnsen 63), Cole, Kezman (Drogba 62), Robben (Duff 46) Unused Substitutes: Pidgeley, Geremi, Terry, Grant	Rene Temmi
7/12	GROUP H: FC PORTO 2 CHELSEA 1	42409
A	Goalscorer: Duff 33 Cech, Gallas, Terry, Carvalho, Ferreira, Smertin (Tiago 65), Lampard, Parker, Bridge, Duff (Robben 54), Drogba (Kezman 77) Unused Substitutes: Cudicini, Makelele, Geremi, Gudjohnsen	Massimo Busacca

23/02		KNOCK-OUT ROUND FIRST LEG: FC BARCELONA 2 CHELSEA 1	89000
A		Goalscorer: Belletti 33 (og) Cech, Terry, Ferreira, Gallas, Carvalho, Makelele, Lampard, Cole (Johnson 70) Duff (Gudjohnsen 76), Tiago (Smertin 90), Drogba Unused Substitutes: Cudicini, Kezman, Geremi, Morais	Anders Frisk
08/03		KNOCK-OUT ROUND SECOND LEG: CHELSEA 4 FC BARCELONA 2	41315
H		Goalscorers: Gudjohnsen 8; Lampard 17; Duff 19; Terry 76 Cech, Ferreira (Johnson 51), Terry, Carvalho, Gallas, Makelele, Cole, Lampard, Duff (Huth 85), Kezman, Gudjohnsen (Tiago 78) Unused Substitutes: Cudicini, Smertin, Geremi, Parker	Pierluigi Collina
06/04		QUARTER-FINAL FIRST LEG: CHELSEA 4 BAYERN MUNICH 2	40253
H		Goalscorers: Cole 5; Lampard 59, 70; Drogba 81 Cech, Johnson (Huth 65), Carvalho, Terry, Gallas, Cole (Tiago 82), Lampard, Makelele, Duff, Gudjohnsen, Drogba (Forssell 89) Unused Substitutes: Cudicini, Smertin, Geremi, Morais	Rene Temmink
12/04		QUARTER-FINAL SECOND LEG: BAYERN MUNICH 3 CHELSEA 2	59000
A		Goalscorers: Lampard 30; Drogba 80 Cech, Carvalho, Huth, Terry, Gallas, Cole (Morais 90), Makelele, Lampard, Duff (Tiago 71), Drogba, Gudjohnsen (Geremi 85) Unused Substitutes: Cudicini, Johnson, Smertin, Forssell	Manuel Mejuto González
27/04		SEMI-FINAL FIRST LEG: CHELSEA 0 LIVERPOOL 0	40497
H		Cech, Johnson, Terry, Carvalho, Gallas, Tiago (Robben 59), Makelele, Lampard, Cole (Kezman 78), Gudjohnsen, Drogba Unused Substitutes: Cudicini, Huth, Smertin, Geremi, Forssell	Alain Sars
03/05		SEMI-FINAL SECOND LEG: LIVERPOOL 1 CHELSEA 0	42529
A		Cech, Carvalho, Terry, Gallas, Geremi (Huth 76), Tiago (Kezman 68), Makelele, Lampard, Cole (Robben 68), Drogba, Gudjohnsen Unused Substitutes: Cudicini, Johnson, Morais, Forssell	Lubos Michel